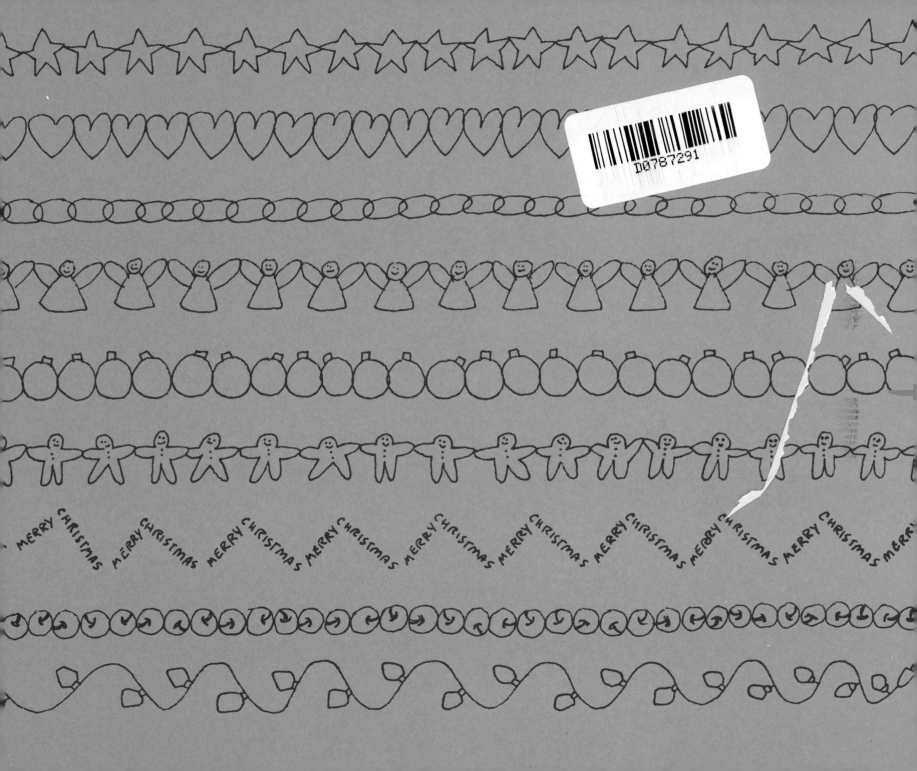

11-6   4⁰⁰

Christmas Counting

by Lynn Reiser

Greenwillow Books New York

TO
BARBARA
ERNEST
NICOLE
AND
MICHAEL

Watercolors and a black pen were used for
the full-color art.
The text type is Century Old Style.

Printed in Singapore by Tien Wah Press
First Edition   10 9 8 7 6 5 4 3 2 1

Library of Congress
Cataloging-in-Publication Data
Reiser, Lynn.
Christmas counting / by Lynn Reiser.
        p.   cm.
Summary:
Ten successive Christmases in
a clearing in the forest witness
the simultaneous growth of a tiny
fir tree and a family.
ISBN 0-688-10676-5.
ISBN 0-688-10677-3 (lib. bdg.)
[1. Christmas—Fiction.
2. Christmas trees—Fiction.
3. Growth—Fiction.
4. Counting.]   I. Title.
PZ7.R27745Ch   1992
[E]—dc20
91-32501   CIP   AC

Once
there was
a clearing in the forest
under the moon shining down.

The first Christmas,
in the clearing in the forest,
there was a very tiny little fir tree.

A man built a house beside it

and brought the tree inside the house
and put
1 star on top of it.

And after Christmas
the man planted
the very tiny little fir tree
back in the clearing in the forest
under the moon shining down.

The second Christmas,
in the clearing in the forest,
there was a very little fir tree.

A groom
carried it inside the house
and put
1 star on top of it—

and a bride put
2 hearts on it.

And after Christmas
the groom planted
the very little fir tree
back in the clearing in the forest
under the moon shining down.

The third Christmas,
in the clearing in the forest,
there was a little fir tree.

A husband
lifted it inside the house
and put
1 star on top of it,
a wife put
2 hearts on it—

and a puppy put
3 paper chains on it.

And after Christmas
the husband planted
the little fir tree
back in the clearing in the forest
under the moon shining down.

The fourth Christmas,
in the clearing in the forest,
there was a bigger little fir tree.

A father
lugged it inside the house
and put
1 star on top of it,
a mother put
2 hearts on it,
a dog put
3 paper chains on it—

and a baby daughter put
4 angels on it.

And after Christmas
the father planted
the bigger little fir tree
back in the clearing in the forest
under the moon shining down.

The fifth Christmas,
in the clearing
in the forest,
there was a big fir tree.

The father
pushed it inside the house
and put
1 star on top of it,
the mother put
2 hearts on it,
the dog put
3 paper chains on it,
a crawling girl put
4 angels on it—

and a kitten put
5 colored balls on it.

And after Christmas
the father planted
the big fir tree
back in the clearing in the forest
under the moon shining down.

The sixth Christmas,
in the clearing in the forest,
there was a very big fir tree.

The father
dragged it
inside the house
and put
1 star on top of it,
the mother put
2 hearts on it,
the dog put
3 paper chains on it,
a walking girl put
4 angels on it,
the cat put
5 colored balls on it—

and a baby son put
6 gingerbread men on it.

And after Christmas
the father planted
the very big fir tree
back in the clearing in the forest
under the moon shining down.

The seventh Christmas,
in the clearing in the forest,
there was
a very great big fir tree.
The father
wheeled it
inside the house
and put
1 star on top of it,
the mother put
2 hearts on it,
the dog put
3 paper chains on it,
a running girl put
4 angels on it,
the cat put
5 colored balls on it,
a crawling boy put
6 gingerbread men on it—
and a parrot greeted it
7 times.

MERRY CHRISTMAS
MERRY CHRISTMAS
MERRY CHRISTMAS
MERRY CHRISTMAS
MERRY CHRISTMAS
MERRY CHRISTMAS
MERRY CHRISTMAS

And after Christmas
the father planted
the very great big fir tree
back in the clearing in the forest
under the moon shining down.

The eighth Christmas,
in the clearing in the forest,
there was
a very great big huge fir tree.

The father pulled it
inside the house
and put
1 star on top of it,

the mother put
2 hearts on it,

the dog put
3 paper chains on it,

a skipping girl put
4 angels on it,

the cat put
5 colored balls on it,

a walking boy put
6 gingerbread men on it,

the parrot
greeted it
7 times—

MERRY CHRISTMAS
MERRY CHRISTMAS
MERRY CHRISTMAS
MERRY CHRISTMAS
MERRY CHRISTMAS
MERRY CHRISTMAS
MERRY CHRISTMAS

and a pony put
8 silver bells on it.

And after Christmas
the father planted
the very great big huge fir tree
back in the clearing in the forest
under the moon shining down.

The ninth Christmas,
in the clearing in the forest,
there was
a very great big huge enormous fir tree.

The father had
1 star
ready.

The mother had
2 hearts
ready.

The girl had
4 angels
ready.

The dog had
3 paper chains
ready.

The cat had
5 colored balls
ready.

The boy had
6 gingerbread men
ready.

The parrot had
7 greetings
ready.

The pony had
8 silver bells
ready.

But there was no tree inside the house.
The father could not budge
the very great big huge enormous fir tree.

It was too big.

But there was
a little fir tree beside it—

so the father
brought
the little fir tree
inside the house.

MERRY CHRISTMAS
MERRY CHRISTMAS
MERRY CHRISTMAS
MERRY CHRISTMAS
MERRY CHRISTMAS
MERRY CHRISTMAS
MERRY CHRISTMAS

The father put
1 star on top of it,
and the mother put
2 hearts on it,
and the dog put
3 paper chains on it,
and a riding girl put
4 angels on it,
and the cat put
5 colored balls on it
(and five kittens under it),
and a running boy put
6 gingerbread men on it,
and the parrot
greeted it
7 times,
and the pony put
8 silver bells on it.
And then—

the father
and the mother
and the dog
and the girl
and the cat
and her kittens
and the boy
and the parrot
and the pony
went out of the house
and into the clearing in the forest
and put
9 strings of lights
on the very great big
huge enormous fir tree

and sang
10 carols to it.

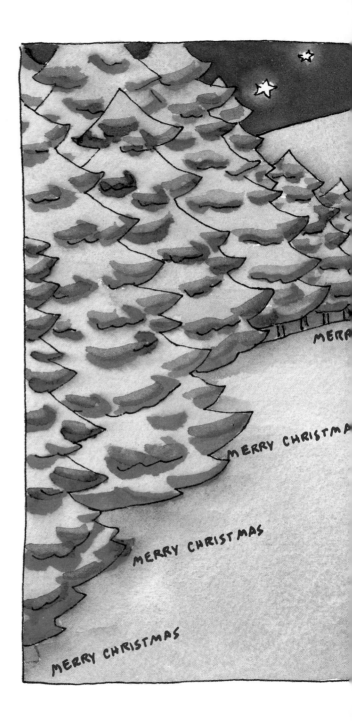

And after Christmas
the father planted the little fir tree back in the clearing in the forest

beside the very great big huge enormous fir tree.

The tenth Christmas
and every Christmas after that,
in the clearing in the forest,
there were big fir trees
and little fir trees,
and a Christmas tree inside
and Christmas trees outside
under the moon shining down.

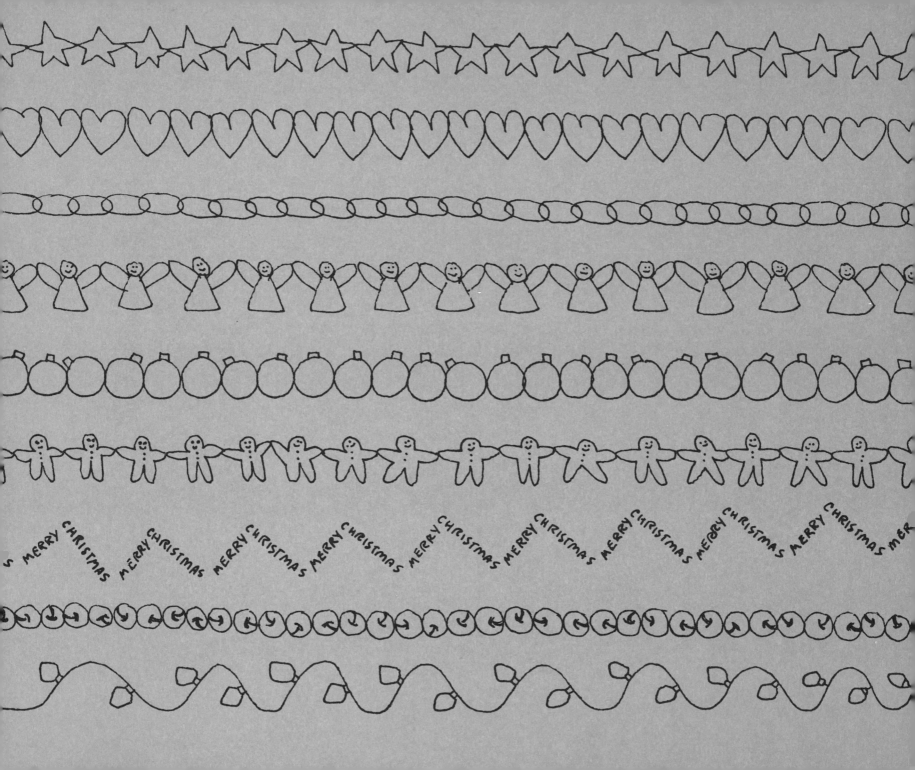